MY FUN WITH
READING

♦

*Stories About
Careers*

MY FUN WITH
READING

BOOK 4

Stories About Careers

SERIES EDITOR
Ronald Kidd

READING CONSULTANTS
Paul E. Stanton, Ph.D.
University of South Carolina, Coastal Carolina College

Ann Lukasevich, Ed.D.
University of British Columbia

THE SOUTHWESTERN COMPANY ■ NASHVILLE, TENNESSEE

RONALD KIDD is owner and Editorial Director of Kidd & Company, Inc., a Nashville-based packager and producer of children's books and records. Previously he held positions as Creative Director, Walt Disney Records, and Editor, Bowmar/Noble Publishers. The published author of seventeen books, he was recipient of the Children's Choice Award, the CINE Golden Eagle, and two Gold Records. He has been nominated for the Edgar Allan Poe Award, the Grammy Award, and the California Young Reader Medal. Mr. Kidd has a secondary teaching credential in English and history.

DR. PAUL E. STANTON completed his Ph.D. at the University of South Carolina in the field of Counseling Psychology, with an emphasis in reading and learning disabilities. He chaired the Department of Reading and Language Arts at the University of Pittsburgh and was co-chair of the Committee on Undergraduate Training in the Teaching of Reading for the International Reading Association (IRA). He was co-developer of the Scholastic *Action* Series, a pioneer high-interest/low-ability reading series produced by Scholastic Book Services. Dr. Stanton served as Vice Chancellor for Academic Affairs at the University of South Carolina, Coastal Carolina College, where he is currently Professor of Psychology specializing in reading and learning disabilities.

DR. ANN LUKASEVICH taught for seventeen years at the elementary school level in Ontario, Canada. She is presently a member of the Language Department at the University of British Columbia, where she originally obtained her Ed.D., and teaches courses in language, reading, early childhood, and curriculum development. She also taught reading and language courses at the University of Calgary for one year and at the University of Western Ontario for three years. During this period, she has done numerous workshops and conference presentations in early childhood education, reading, and language in Canada and the United States. She spent a year in Britain studying British education, and was awarded an advanced Diploma in Child Development. Her interests include parent involvement, evaluation, literacy development, and computer education.

SERIES DESIGN   Bruce Gore
PAGE DESIGN AND ART PRODUCTION   Schatz + Schatz
COVER PHOTOS   Susan Steinkamp/SABA (top)
                 Stephen McBrady (center)
                 George Haling/Photo Researchers (bottom)

CONTENTS

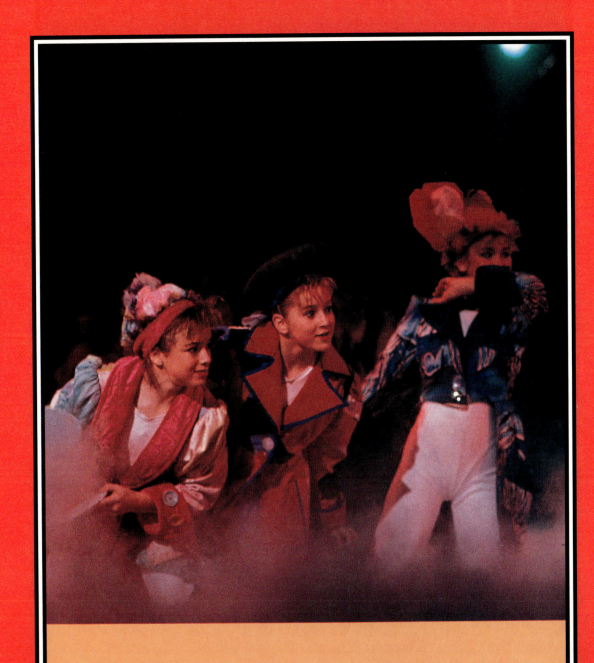

Circus Kids

by LUCINDA CHODAN

If you need help
with hard words,
please turn to p. 36.

PHOTOGRAPHS:

Susan Steinkamp/SABA pp. 7, 9-27, 35, 36
Jean-Francois Leblanc/Agence Stock Photo pp. 28-34
ILLUSTRATIONS: Joel Snyder
We gratefully acknowledge the cooperation of Cirque du Soleil.

Faon practices a headstand.

What comes to your mind when you think of school? Maybe you imagine yourself at a desk, watching your teacher at the blackboard.

School is different for Faon Bélanger and her friends Corrine, Noémie, and Annie. The four girls belong to a circus troupe. Along with their arithmetic and spelling, they practice headstands and trampoline jumps.

Corrine on the trampoline

Faon puts on her costume.

That's not the only difference between their school and yours. You walk, ride, or take the bus to your school. Faon and her friends take their school with them wherever they go. They might have lessons in four or five cities in one school year.

Their teachers travel with the circus as it moves from city to city and from country to country. Sometimes the classroom is outside in the sunshine. And sometimes it's under the big black-and-white tent where the circus performers practice.

Faon and her friends are members of the Cirque du Soleil. The name is French for "Circus of the Sun." Every night, the girls put on colorful makeup and bright costumes. Then they perform breathtaking tricks for hundreds of people who come to the big Cirque du Soleil tent.

Faon is twelve years old. She wears a red costume and dances with the grownup performers in the show. Her friends Annie and Corrine ride a bicycle around the tent. That doesn't sound too hard — until you realize that they're both riding the same bicycle. So are eleven other people!

Noémie has to have a good sense of balance for her trick. She climbs to the top of a tower of chairs that is about twelve feet high. When she gets to the top, she throws her arms into the air to show she isn't afraid.

Annie, Corrine, and friends

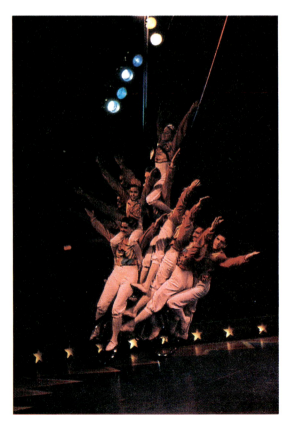

The Cirque du Soleil isn't like most circuses. There are no lions or tigers or elephants. In fact, there are no animals at all.

Sometimes the Cirque du Soleil looks and sounds more like a rock concert than a circus. The band that travels with the circus plays rock music during the show. Often the people in the circus dance and perform in a fog of dry ice, the way rock stars sometimes do.

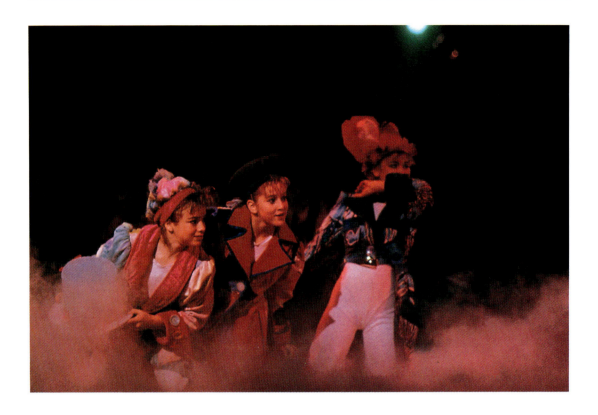

Faon, Corrine, Noémie, and Annie are among people from around the world who perform in the Cirque du Soleil. The four girls are all from Canada, the home of the circus. But there are also people from the United States, Bulgaria, and France. Talking to the other performers is almost like a geography lesson!

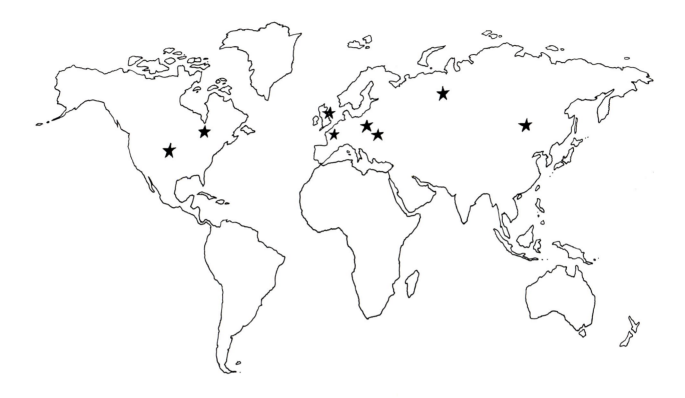

Vassiliy Demenchoukov is an acrobat and a juggler. He and his friend Vladimir Kehkaial were acrobats in the Soviet Union. They came all the way from Moscow to join the circus.

Wang Hong also had to travel far to be part of the Cirque du Soleil. Her home is in China. She learned to be a juggler in a Chinese circus.

There are also five French trapeze artists, two acrobats from Poland, and a tightrope walker from England. When the whole troupe meets, there can be conversations in five or six languages going on at once!

Most of the circus troupe members are adults. But each year, there are at least three or four children under the "big top" — that's what circus people call the large tent where they perform.

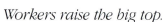

Workers raise the big top.

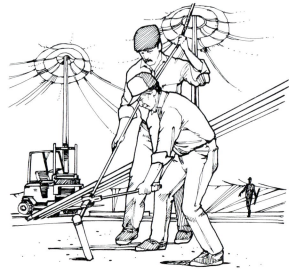

Faon and her friends are acrobats. They know how to do perfect cartwheels and backflips. They also know how to jump off the end of what looks like a seesaw and do a somersault in the air. When they put on their sparkling costumes and do their show under the big top, the crowd cheers and claps.

Crowds all over the world love the circus. Faon and her friends have performed their act in the United States and Canada.

It's an exciting life. It's also hard work. Each morning, the girls meet with their tutor, a special teacher who goes wherever the circus goes. The tutor teaches the young acrobats and the children of the adult performers.

Faon and her tutor

Faon and her friends study two languages, French and English, plus all the other school subjects. They have tests and reports, just as you do. After meeting with the tutor, the girls might go to their trailers to write a letter or do some homework.

Then they spend the afternoon practicing their circus acts. This practice is another kind of homework. Circus performers are like ballet dancers or athletes training for the Olympics. If they don't practice at least two hours a day, their bodies will get stiff. Then they might not be able to perform the difficult tricks they do in the show each night.

Corrine in her trailer

Circus performers practice so much they can do things that look almost impossible. One of the adults in the Cirque du Soleil is a contortionist — someone who can twist her body into odd shapes. At times, she looks like a human pretzel!

Faon and her friends are young. But they've already been training for years to be part of the circus. Faon knew when she was only six that she wanted to be an acrobat. She started doing gymnastics as practice that same year. Since she's twelve now, that means she's been training to be in the circus for half of her life.

Faon and most of the other children who are in the Cirque du Soleil trained at a special circus school in Montreal. About 165 young people come to the school each year to learn about performing.

They take courses in juggling and clowning and trapeze. They learn how to do acrobatic tricks without getting hurt. It sounds like fun — until you have to do it for five or six hours a day. Instead of a test at the end of the year, the children perform the tricks they've learned for an audience that comes to the school.

Some of the best students in the circus school, like Faon, go on to join the Cirque du Soleil. But even there they never really stop studying. Though they already have special parts to play in the show, they're always working on something new.

Faon "studying"

At the afternoon practices, Faon and her friends try out new tricks. They also do the old ones over and over again to make them even better. That might mean doing the same somersault fifteen or twenty times to make sure it's just right.

After the children rehearse, they take a break to eat supper. Meals are served in the canteen, a big kitchen that travels with the circus.

Everyone lives and eats and plays together — for months at a time when the circus is on tour. That makes being part of the Cirque du Soleil almost like being part of a family. But it's a family in which you have eighty or ninety aunts and uncles and brothers and sisters!

Annie (left) *and friend in canteen*

After the supper break, it's time to get ready for the show. The girls put on makeup, so even the people sitting far away can see their faces. They carefully put on their costumes. They might take a minute to rehearse a dance step one last time. Then they wait for the music that means the show is starting. When the band starts, the circus magic begins.

Noémie gets ready for the show.

The first group of acrobats races into the ring, the part of the tent where the performances take place. They dance and wave to the crowd as the band plays the Cirque du Soleil songs. In the next 2½ hours, all the performers do the tricks they've been practicing so hard.

Corrine and Noémie resting
before the show

Vassiliy comes into the tent. He sits down at a table covered with a tablecloth. Is he going to eat dinner? Not exactly. He puts one chair on top of the table, then another, then another. Finally there are eight chairs stacked on top of each other. Then Vassiliy does a one-handed handstand at the top of the stack, holding a cake in his other hand!

Vassiliy Demenchoukov

Next comes his friend Vladimir. Vladimir walks slowly into the big top and wraps two thick ropes around his arms. The ropes are attached to a pulley at the top of the tent. There are four circus helpers holding on to the other end. As Vladimir runs in a large circle, the helpers — known as La Corporation — pull on the ropes. As he runs, he lifts off the ground like a bird taking flight. The crowd gasps. Vladimir is flying!

La Corporation

Wang Hong's trick looks simple. She has nothing with her in the ring except a chair, two red and pink umbrellas, and four small rugs. First she twirls the umbrellas with her toes, tossing them up in the air and catching them with her feet. Then she makes the rugs spin on her fingertips and her toes as if they were flying carpets.

Wang Hong

Now it's the turn of the young contortionists.
Nadine Binette and her friends twist and turn their
legs and arms and backs together until they look like
a rope with lots of knots in it!

The French acrobats fly through the air on their trapezes. One of Faon's friends does a somersault on the tightrope. People dance on stilts that reach nearly to the top of the tent. And of course there are always the clowns. Before you know it, the show is over.

On the tightrope

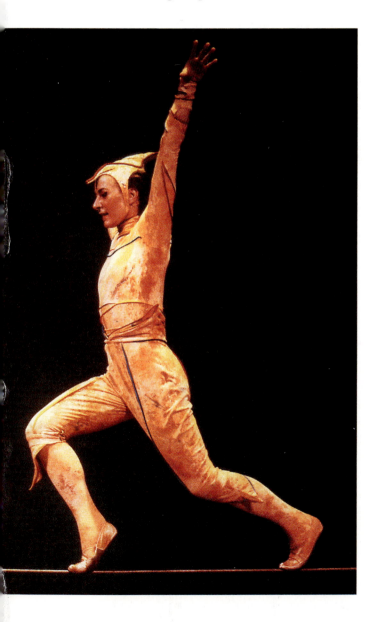

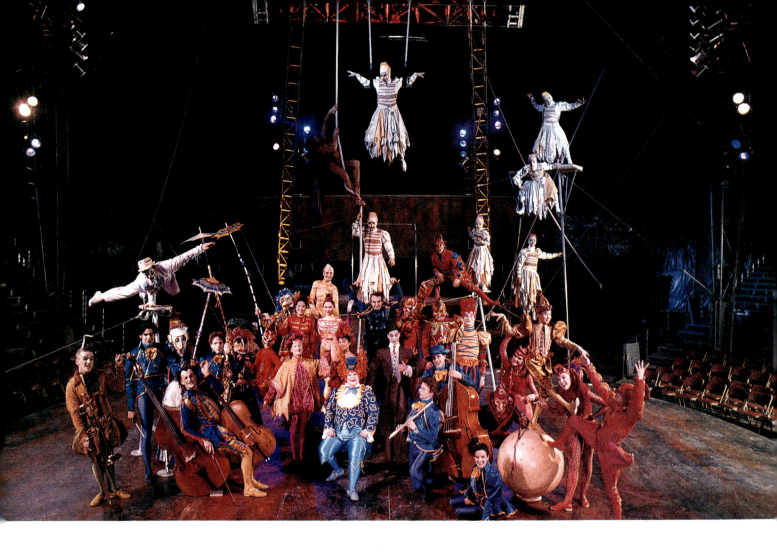

The crowd claps and shouts and whistles as the performers smile and bow. The applause of the crowd makes all the hard work and practice seem worthwhile.

Then Faon and her friends hurry off to bed. They have another long day of school and practice ahead of them before the magic of the circus can start again tomorrow night.

Annie and her mother after the show

What Does It Mean?

acrobats: people who can twist and move their bodies in strange or different ways

breathtaking: amazing, hard to believe

conversation: talk

geography: the study of places around the world

rehearse: to practice

somersault: a head-over-heels turn

How Do You Say It?

Bulgaria: buhl GEHR ee ah

Cirque du Soleil: SEERK dew so LAY

Corinne: ko RINN

Faon Bélanger: FAHN bay lahn JAY

gymnastics: jim NAS ticks

Montreal: mahn tree ALL

Moscow: MAHSS kow

Noémie: no ay MEE

Olympics: oh LIM picks

Vassiliy Demenchoukov: vah SEE lee deh men CHOO kov

Vladimir Kehkaial: vlah DEE meer keh KIE uhl

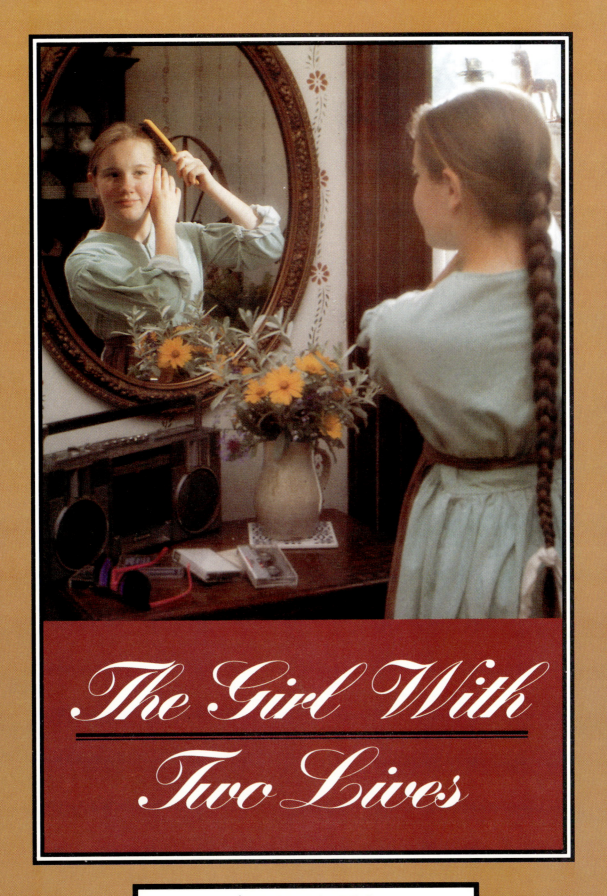

The Girl With Two Lives

by RONALD KIDD

*If you need help
with hard words,
please turn to p. 66.*

PHOTOGRAPHS: Stephen McBrady

ILLUSTRATIONS: Joel Snyder

We gratefully acknowledge the cooperation of Conner Prairie, an Earlham Museum.

The year is 1836. In an Indiana frontier village, Sally Johnson sweeps off the porch of the Golden Eagle Inn. The inn is a friendly place where travelers can stop for food and a night's rest.

After sweeping, Sally draws water from the well. Then she goes inside to help prepare the noon meal. The innkeeper, Martha Zimmerman, watches her set the table to make sure things are done properly.

In the pantry, Sally slices carrots and potatoes to make a stew. She cooks them in a kettle over the fire, because there's no stove. There are no electric

Innkeeper Martha Zimmerman (right) *watches Sally set the table.*

lights and no refrigerator. If you told her about such things, she would probably laugh and say you'd been out in the sun too long.

And yet here's someone who looks very much like Sally Johnson, cutting up vegetables by the light of an electric lamp. Behind her are a stove and refrigerator. She's wearing jeans and modern-day glasses. When she smiles, we see braces on her teeth. Who is she?

She's a girl with two lives.

In this life her name is Penny McDowell. She and her parents live in a suburb of Indianapolis, Indiana. Penny likes rock groups and movie stars. She does homework and watches TV. She plays French horn in the band. And she has one very unusual hobby.

Several days a week Penny puts on rough, old-fashioned clothes and goes to Conner Prairie, a living museum of the American frontier. There she steps into her other life as Sally Johnson, pioneer girl.

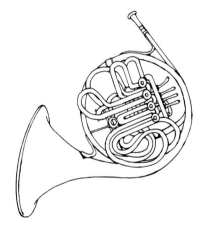

For Penny, the role of Sally Johnson is more than just a hobby. It's almost a way of life. She grew up in and around Conner Prairie, because her mother worked there, playing the parts of other frontier characters. Even at home, Penny is surrounded by things from the past. There are quilts and antique furniture. There are old clocks and a tin wash basin. The house itself is over a hundred years old.

Penny's mother makes all the clothes she and her daughter wear at Conner Prairie. When Penny tries on a dress, you might almost mistake her for Sally Johnson — if you didn't notice the stereo earphones.

Penny is what's known as an *interpreter.* She interprets, or helps people understand, what frontier life was like. It's an important job in a very different type of museum.

At Conner Prairie, visitors don't just read or hear about history. They walk down the dusty streets of a frontier town. They explore an authentic barn and schoolhouse and store. Everywhere they go, they brush shoulders with characters from the past. One of them is Sally Johnson.

"How much do you charge for lunch?" they ask as she puts a kettle on the fire.

"Oh, do you mean the noonday meal?" she says. "Around these parts, we call it dinner. It costs twenty-five cents. But it's worth every penny."

A man enters with his wife and young son. "What are the beds like?" he asks.

"Good and clean. Only a few bed bugs," she says. "We've still got one bed left for tonight. That should do for the three of you."

A little girl giggles. "How often do you take a bath?"

"Once a week," Sally answers, "whether I need it or not."

For these visitors, history may never be the same.

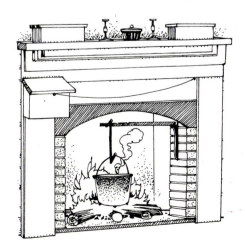

To learn about Sally, Penny McDowell goes to the museum library. She reads magazines of the time. She checks out books and articles about nineteenth century life. She might glance at an information sheet that gives facts about Sally's life.

The character of Sally Johnson was made up by the people at the museum, based on their findings about real frontier girls. Sally lives on a farm outside of town with her parents, Luke and Sarah Johnson. The family came to Indiana from Kentucky in 1823. Sally doesn't remember the trip, because she was still a baby.

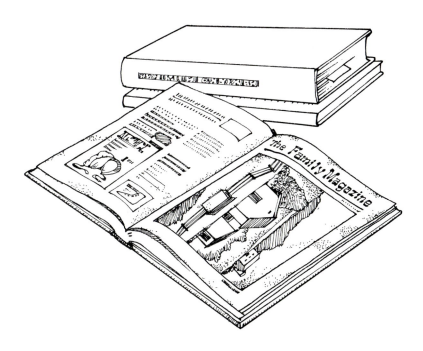

Sally works at the Golden Eagle Inn to pay off her father's debt. When she's not at the inn, she helps care for her little brother and sister. She might even take a turn in the fields next to her father and older brother.

Life is hard in 1836, but Sally finds time to play, too. Visitors are often surprised to see her running down the road, pushing a metal hoop in front of her. It's a game pioneer children used to play.

Sally can barely read and write. Still, she
sometimes goes to school with the other children
in town. All ages attend, from seven to seventeen.

YOU ARE ENTERING
PRAIRIETOWN.
THE YEAR IS 1836.

Schoolmaster Caleb Ferguson

Waiting at the door is the schoolmaster, Caleb Ferguson. When he's not teaching, he has a business making and repairing harnesses. Mr. Ferguson is a stern but kindly man. He drills the children in reading, writing, arithmetic, and history.

Seth Bucher

After school, Sally runs some errands for Mrs. Zimmerman. This is her favorite part of the day, because she gets to visit her friends in town.

At Whitaker's store, she buys a few supplies from the clerk, Seth Bucher, then gazes longingly at some rock candy. Before leaving, she takes a moment to watch Katie Bend and Molly Cox play checkers.

Up the street is a familiar-looking face. It's Penny McDowell's mother! But to Sally Johnson, this woman is the doctor's wife, Harriet Campbell. Hearing the two of them talk, you'd never know that in Sally's other life they are mother and daughter.

Harriet Campbell

Katie Bend and Molly Cox

Doctor's apprentice Peter Dale

Dr. Campbell is out seeing patients today. But Peter Dale is in the office. Peter is the doctor's helper, or *apprentice*. He's surrounded by strange-looking medical tools and cures of the day.

The ladies' literary society

Sally peeks into the Campbells' parlor. There, some young visitors are watching a meeting of the ladies' literary society. These well-dressed women gather once a month to discuss books, magazines, and the latest fashions.

As Sally leaves, old Samuel Hastings spots her. Before she can escape, he launches into a story about his adventures in the War of 1812.

At the end of the lane, blacksmith Ben Curtis takes a break from the anvil. He gets a drink of water and calls out a greeting to Sally as she walks by.

Samuel Hastings

The blacksmith's shop

Ben's wife Mary asks Sally to come inside and give her a hand. While Mary spins yarn on the spinning wheel, Sally gathers it up and wraps it on a device known as a knitty knotty.

Mary Curtis

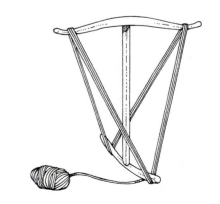

Knitty knotty

Grace Fenton at her loom

On her way back to the inn, Sally passes the weaver's house. Inside, museum visitors learn what happens to yarn after it's spun. Using a big wooden loom, Grace Fenton weaves together yarns of different colors to form a rug.

Across the way, carpenter Daniel McClure shows how he uses a shaving horse to make a table leg. The children who watch are eager to try it themselves. Conner Prairie has just the place for them. It's called the Pioneer Adventure Area.

Here, guests can climb onto a shaving horse to see how it works. They can weave, quilt, spin, dip candles, and make soap. When they've finished their activities in that area, they can take a walk on a nature trail, or visit the 1823 estate of William Conner, for whom the museum was named.

Daniel McClure

The Pioneer Adventure Area

Returning to the village in a horse-drawn wagon, guests see Sally Johnson going about her chores at the Golden Eagle Inn. It's been a long day for the hard-working frontier girl. She still has to make the beds and air out the mattresses. Afterwards she takes a moment to feed the horses.

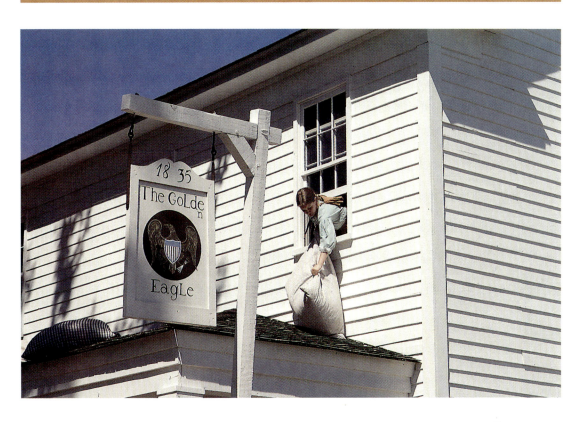

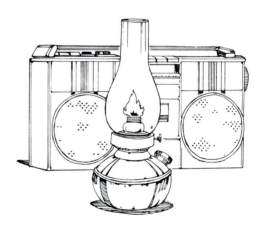

Later that evening, in a very different world, Penny McDowell phones a girlfriend and watches TV. Her mother braids her hair. Then Penny heads off to bed. As she lies in the darkness, she thinks about all her friends at Conner Prairie, and she smiles.

Sally Johnson smiles right along with her.

What Does It Mean?

errand: a short trip to do something

estate: a large house and the land that goes with it

kettle: a big, heavy pot

mattress: a pad on which people sleep

nineteenth century: the 1800s

old-fashioned: of years past

pantry: a room or closet in which food is kept

porch: the covered front of a building

quilt: a bed cover made of cloth squares

suburb: an area just outside the city

How Do You Say It?

antique: an TEEK

century: SEN cher ee

character: KAR ik ter

debt: DETT

earphone: IHR fone

frontier: frahn TEER

Indianapolis: in dee uh NAP uh luss

magazine: mag uh ZEEN

PROJECT:
What I Want to Be

by YVONNE MARTIN

If you need help
with hard words,
please turn to p. 96.

PHOTOGRAPHS:

Stephen McBrady pp. 69, 72, 75, 77, 82 (left), 86, 87, 90 (right), 95, 96
Blair Seitz/Photo Researchers p. 73
Joe Munroe/Photo Researchers p. 74
Tom Hollyman/Photo Researchers pp. 76, 91
George Haling/Photo Researchers pp. 67, 78, 79
Junebug Clark/Photo Researchers p. 80
Paul Shambroom/Photo Researchers pp. 81, 83
Will/Deni McIntyre/Photo Researchers p. 82 (right)
Tomas d.w. Friedmann/Photo Researchers p. 84
Susan Leavines/Photo Researchers p. 85
Joseph Nettis/Photo Researchers pp. 88, 94
William A. Graham/Photo Researchers p. 89
Renee Lynn/Photo Researchers p. 90
James Foote/Photo Researchers p. 92
Allen Green/Photo Researchers p. 93

ILLUSTRATIONS: Joel Snyder

Take a close look. That's me — the one on your far right with the suit neatly pressed, the briefcase at my side, and the confident look of a man dressed for success.

You might be wondering what the five of us are doing dressed up like this. It isn't Halloween. And we certainly don't wear these clothes to school every day.

Today we're presenting our team project to Mr. Green's fifth grade class at Franklin School.

Four weeks ago, Mr. Green chose teams and gave each team a different assignment. Ours was to think about the future and present our ideas to the class.

At first we thought of really strange things. Automobiles that would fly. Robots that would do your homework. A pepperoni pizza in the form of a pill.

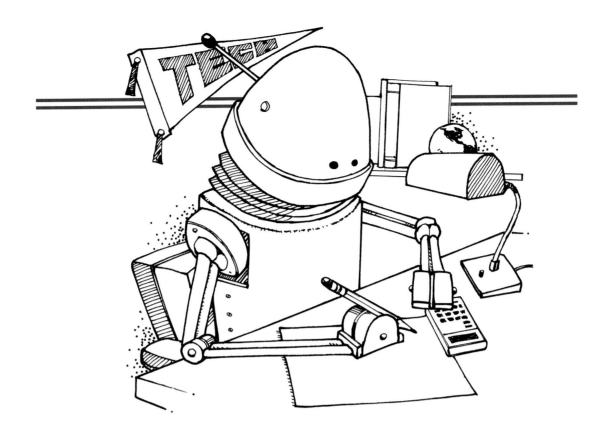

But then we decided to look a little closer to home. Instead of thinking about what would happen a hundred years from now, we decided to look at the near future. What would each of us be doing in fifteen or twenty years?

We would call our project "What I Want to Be." Each of us would read about and present careers that interested us.

That's how it started. Here's where it ended a month later. Jim, Maria, Stephanie, Cathy, and me, Eric, dressed up like a construction worker, doctor, ballerina, police officer, and business executive.

Say hi to Maria. She's as smart as she looks. She especially loves to study tough subjects like math and science. Maria wondered what it might be like to have a job using those skills.

If you like people and don't faint at the sight of blood, you might want to be a doctor. A doctor works with patients to find out why they feel bad, then treats them with medicine or surgery. Doctors also like to see patients who are well, to help them stay healthy.

Doctor

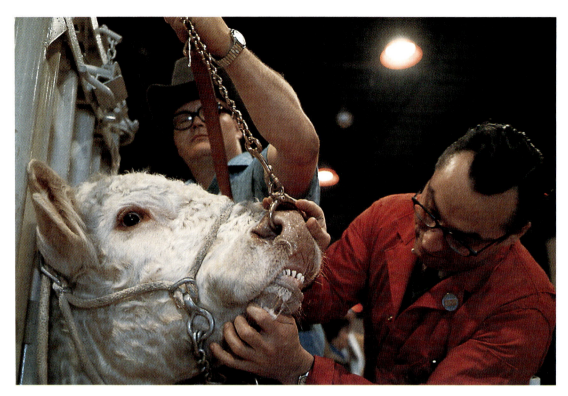

Veterinarian

A veterinarian is a doctor, too. But instead of boys and girls, a vet's patients might be cows and goats. Like doctors, vets diagnose disease and give treatment. Although many vets deal only with small animals like dogs, cats, and birds, many treat larger farm animals, such as horses and sheep.

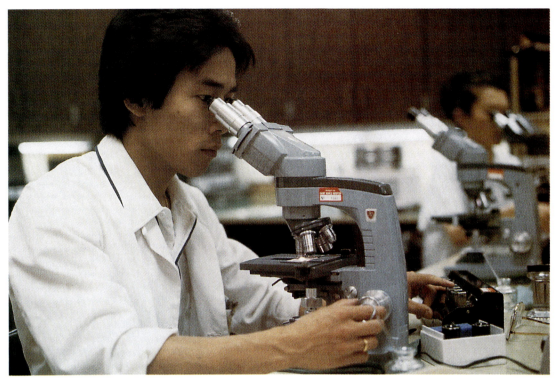

Biochemist

Would you enjoy working in a laboratory and watching tiny creatures through a microscope? Then you should consider a career as a biochemist. Biochemists conduct lab experiments and study organisms that you and I can't see with the bare eye. As a biochemist, you might discover a cure for the common cold or a way to improve the food we eat.

If you like math problems and using the computer for things other than playing games, you might think about a career as a mathematician. You could work for a large company to help keep track of the business. Or you could be a math professor and teach at a college. Either way, your days would be spent trying to solve math puzzles.

Mathematician

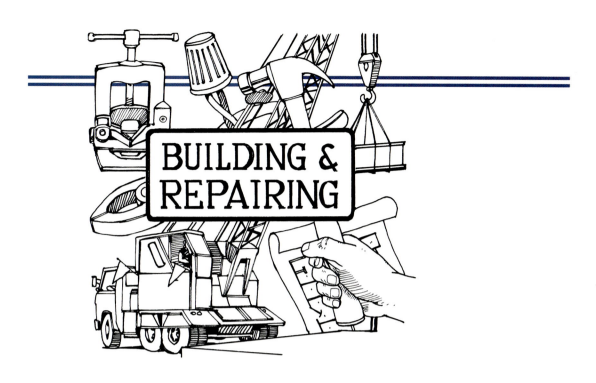

Here's Jim. As you may have guessed from the picture, he loves to work with his hands. He builds things such as tree houses and model cars. He also enjoys helping his dad with "fix it" projects around the house. Jim reported on four careers he might enjoy.

Drafter

Before anything gets built — a car, an office building, a piece of equipment — somebody needs to draw the plan. A drafter works with architects, engineers, scientists, or designers to turn the ideas into drawings that can easily be followed. The final drawings show what the item should look like from all sides.

Think of the challenge of building a twenty-story office building! The building contractor is the person who coordinates the activities of all the people involved: electricians, plumbers, carpenters, and many other workers. Because of bad weather and other delays, this job takes patience and determination to keep projects on schedule.

Machinists use sharp cutting tools to grind and shape metal into almost anything — parts for cars, airplanes, and equipment. Any error, even the size of a hair, could cause a problem. Machinists must wear earplugs, special glasses, and heavy aprons to protect them from noise and flying metal.

Machinist

Computers help run every kind of business, from the federal government to the corner market. But have you ever thought about what happens when a computer breaks down? Computer service technicians keep large computer systems running. They don't wait until the computer stops. Instead, they visit their electronic "patients" on a regular basis to prevent trouble.

Computer service technician

Cathy wants a job serving and protecting the public. She reported on careers in which she could do just that.

A teacher is responsible for helping kids like us develop into good citizens. Teachers try to give students individual attention to help them learn the basic skills and knowledge they will need later in life. Many parents find teaching a good career, since the hours and vacation schedules are the same as their children's.

Teacher

Fire fighter

A fire fighter must be strong and brave. And, because fire fighters live together for days at a time, they need to get along well with other people. At the scene of a fire, some connect hoses to fire hydrants. Others put up ladders or manage the water pumps. Between alarms, fire fighters spend time practicing their skills and cleaning and repairing the equipment.

Police officers sometimes face danger, but not all their work is the "cops and robbers" kind that you see on television. Some police officers have less dangerous jobs, such as identifying fingerprints, analyzing handwriting, and directing crowds or traffic.

Police officer

If you've ever been on an airplane, you've experienced the work of an air traffic controller. These are the people who track the movements of all the planes in an area. Air traffic controllers have to make quick decisions and give clear instructions. They must also have excellent eyesight.

Air traffic controller

Stephanie, our team's ballerina, is very creative. At times you can catch her staring off into space, thinking about a story to write, a picture to draw, or a new way of entertaining her family and friends. Stephanie entertained us with several careers.

Do you daydream, the way Stephanie does? Most artists do. They love creating what they have imagined. Some artists draw or paint. Some sculpt or carve figures out of rock and clay. There's no limit to what an artist can do, because there's no limit to the imagination.

Ballet, anyone? Professional dancers make it look easy, because they practice many hours each day. Some dancers like to perform in public. Some *choreograph,* or compose dances for others. Still others choose to teach in public or private schools.

Sculptor

Dancers

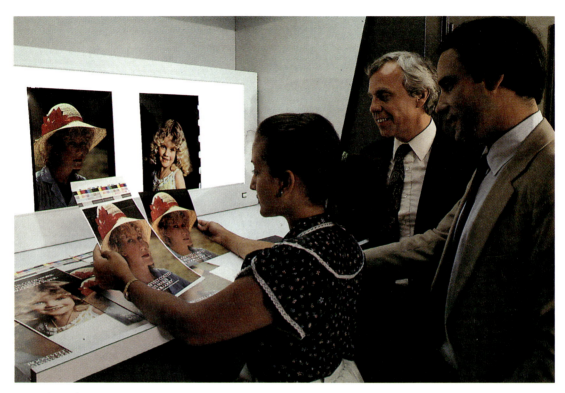

Graphic designer

Have you ever wondered who is responsible for the "look" of your favorite poster, book, or magazine? Graphic designers sketch out their ideas, then get photographs, illustrations, or computer images that bring their sketches to life. A graphic designer watches over the final printing of the project to make sure the colors are just right.

Musicians

If you don't like practicing, you probably wouldn't want to be a professional musician. Depending on what instruments they play, musicians might be in a symphony orchestra, or in a rock, jazz, or country group. Since most performances take place at night, musicians work when most other people are home.

The next time you open a morning newspaper, consider what it's like to be a writer. Newspaper writers interview people and attend events to collect the information they need for an accurate story. Because papers come out every day, most newspaper writers must work quickly.

Here I am again. Like my dad, I want an important job downtown, helping to run a business. I like the idea of dressing up each day, looking sharp, and carrying my briefcase to the office.

One career I looked at was banker. Bankers help families and businesses manage their money. In addition, if people need money to buy a car or house, a banker can lend it to them. As you may have guessed, bankers need to be very honest, since they work with other people's money.

Banker

Accountant

Accountants keep track of how much money a company makes and how much it spends. Just like us, a company's goal is to have "allowance" money left over at the end of the week to save for things it really wants.

I might want to be an attorney. On TV, lawyers are usually trying to convince the judge and jury that their clients are innocent. These lawyers are criminal attorneys. Another type of attorney specializes in business law. This person prepares contracts and helps companies understand laws that affect their business.

Attorneys

Rather than go to work for someone else, I'm also thinking of starting my own business someday. But being a small business owner is hard work. You hire and train your employees, keep track of the money, make and sell your product, even sweep the floors and turn off the lights at night!

Small business owner

Well, that's it for our presentation on careers. But before we go, we want you to meet Joshua, the sixth member of our team. He's the one behind the camera. Joshua not only took our pictures; he found the photos of each career.

Maybe you saw a career that interested you. If you did, you might want to read more about it. Then Joshua will be glad to come over and take your picture, too.

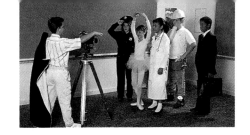

What Does It Mean?

construction: the act of building

coordinate: to cause people or things to work together

determination: the ability or power to work toward a goal

entertain: to put on a show

executive: one who runs or manages a business

individual: a single person or thing

interview: to talk to someone in order to get information

laboratory: a place in which tests and experiments are run

organism: a living thing

How Do You Say It?

assignment: uh SINE ment

determination: dih ter min AY shun

handwriting: HAN drite ing

patient: PAY shunt

pizza: PEET suh

schedule: SKEJ uhl

specialize: SPESH uh lize

symphony orchestra: SIM fuh nee OR kuh struh